HOW TO GROW PALMS

ROSALIND CRAIG & SALLY FRY

A Perigee Book

Perigee Books
are published by
The Putnam Publishing Group
200 Madison Avenue
New York, NY 10016

First American Edition 1987

Library of Congress Cataloging-in-Publication Data

Craig, Rosalind.
  How to read palms.

  "A Perigee book."
  Bibliography: p.
  Reprint. Originally published: Destiny: how to read
your own hand. Wauwatosa, Wis.?: Virgin Books, 1986.
  1. Palmistry. I. Fry, Sally. II. Title.
BF921.C73   1987   133.6   87-6927
ISBN 0-399-51387-6

Printed in the United States of America
1   2   3   4   5   6   7   8   9   10

CONTENTS

SALLY FRY is an international Palm Reader to the famous and infamous, royalty and the public at large. She has tried to adapt the ancient art of Chiromancy (study of the lines of the hand) to modern-day living, helping people with their problems and assessing their potential. She is an honest woman and believes that life is for living. Thus, with her expertise in this field, she hopes to help and guide people to understand themselves a little better, so that they in turn can make the most of what life has to offer.

ROSALIND CRAIG is the mother of three teenage children, a Marriage Guidance Counsellor and a Magistrate in that order! She has been involved in the practice of Palmistry for a number of years and her knowledge of the subject has been invaluable in all aspects of her work.

To Sam

'HE SEALS UP THE HAND OF EVERY MAN
THAT ALL MEN MAY KNOW HIS WORK'

Job 37.7

INTRODUCTION

This book is written for all people as an easy approach to understanding the secrets of the palm and fingers. It is to intrigue, amuse and share with your friends and to give an insight into your negative, as well as positive, qualities; and to a certain extent to help direct you to your own Destiny.

There is no better way to learn the true nature of individuals than by studying palmistry. Discover who are the Leaders in Life, who are the Faithful, the Good or Bad Lovers, the Introvert or the Extrovert simply by scrutinizing their palm.

The science of palmistry is said to date back almost to the creation of time and the human body has always been looked upon as a means of foreseeing omens and portents.

Palmistry can be divided into two main areas: CHIROGNOMY, which deals with the basic character and potential reflected by the size, shape and outward appearance of the hand; and CHIROMANCY, the ability to predict past, present and future from the lines and signs on the palm itself.

DERMATOGLYPHICS is the name given to the study of the skin ridges and patterns covering the palm and fingers. This system is used throughout the world by the police to identify fingerprint patterns.

When analysing or reading a palm it is essential to remember that the subject is very vulnerable. Great care must be taken to use the information in a positive and constructive way.

As you use this book, your skill will improve. You should always limit your readings to what you have learnt. Don't attempt to make guesses. Reading palms is much more a question of a skill to acquire than an intuitive ability.
Used carefully and intelligently, palmistry is a fine way to judge character, health and potential.

PALMISTRY – AN ANCIENT SCIENCE

The use of hand prints can be traced back to early Stone Age cave drawings. As far back as 563 BC it was noted that Buddha had certain markings on his feet which were proof of his greatness, and it is believed that palmistry was first recognised in Europe around the time of Alexander the Great. Fingerprints were often used instead of signatures and in China the Emperor's thumb print was used on State documents. In 1595 a book was published by Joannes Rothmann entitled *Chiromantiea Theorica Practica* and in 1661 a collection of writings on Chirology appeared which incorporated over 70 books on the subject.

One of the best-known palmists was Count Louis Hamon, who was better known by the name of 'Cheiro', meaning hand. He was the author of several books on the subject which mainly followed the theories of two well-established authorities, D'Arpentigny and Desbarrolles. D'Arpentigny was born in March 1798 and his first book, *La Chirognomia*, published in 1839, caused a new wave of interest in the form of the hand. Desbarrolles was born in August 1801 in Paris and it was his study of the Kaballa (the mystical Hebrew theosophy which flourished between the twelfth and sixteenth centuries) that led him to record his chirological findings in a highly detailed system of classification with fine illustrations of the palm.

Another important contributor to the scientific study of the hand was Dr. Carl Gustav Carus, personal physician to the King of Saxony, who during the mid nineteenth century published several books on the subject. His theory was that the human hand was a cross between a fin and a wing, and that the palm was the elementary part of the hand from which the fingers grew. He saw the palm as the key to the subconscious and the fingers, developing parallel with the thought processes and the key to the conscious mind. Hands were classified into two types: the first was the prehensive – those best adapted to the sense of touch – which was subdivided into two further types, the elementary and motoric. The second was the sensitive and psychic. Carus used these classifications to identify the various levels of intellect.

Today, hand analysis has a role to play in medical and psychological diagnosis, a vocational function and the ability to provide a personal analysis. All these possibilities are a direct result of the findings of many years of intensive study by people all over the world.

HOW TO TAKE HAND AND FINGER PRINTS

If you want to undertake a thorough study of your hands, you should take prints. If you are only doing it for fun, a magnifying glass can be used, although this will not give such accurate results as a print.

To take prints you will need: a roller (as used in lino work), fingerprint ink (water-based), a pane of glass or the inside of a biscuit-tin lid – something with a completely smooth surface – a small rubber pad large enough to fit under the narrow part of the palm, tissues, magnifying glass, ruler and paper.

Method: place a sheet of paper with the rubber pad beneath it on a flat table. Squeeze a small amount of ink onto the glass (or other smooth surface) and roll the roller backwards and forwards in the ink until the roller is evenly covered. You are now ready to take the print. The help of another person would be an advantage at this stage. They should take the roller and roll it evenly over the whole of your palm and fingers. Relax your hand and place it down on the paper in the most comfortable position. The other person should then press down on the back of the whole hand. Take your hand off carefully so as not to smudge the ink, and you should have a clear print.

Once a print has been taken, it should be dated immediately and, if it is not your own hand, it should be identified either by a name or by a code number, if the owner objects to their name being used. It can be quite an interesting exercise to take further prints in future years and to ascertain the changes that have taken place.

●CHIROGNOMY●

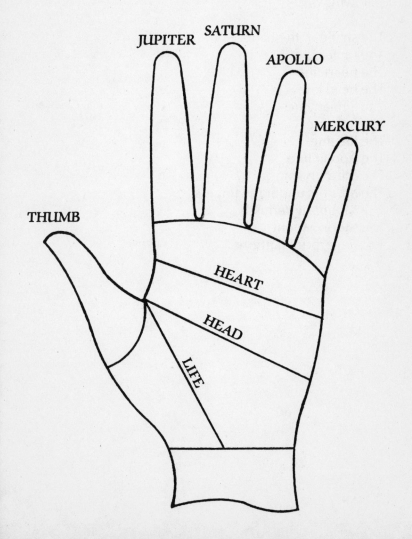

HOW TO ANALYSE THE HAND

The hand and its various aspects are dealt with in the following order:

The shape of the hand
The fingers
The heart line
The head line
The Simian line
The fate line
The life line
The Apollo line
The Mercury line
The Mounts under the fingers
The Mount of Venus
The Moon Mount
The fingerprint patterns

MASCULINE AND FEMININE HANDS

It is possible to assess the proportion of male and female within a human being from their hand. When you are considering the whole hand, the fact that the hand looks delicate does not necessarily mean that the person is particularly feminine. The same with the male – a strong, sturdy hand does not necessarily indicate a masculine personality.

Generally speaking, the round shaping on the hands and fingers suggests female attributes, whereas square shapings on the hands and fingers suggests masculine attributes.

As for the lines on the palm, the straighter the horizontal lines are the more female the personality, and the more curves the more masculine.

A line dropping from the end of the heart line to the head line suggests homosexual tendencies.

THE SHAPE OF THE HAND

There are several basic types of hand shapes: the square, the conical, the knotty, the pointed and the spatulate. There are additional shapes, namely the elementary and the mixed hand, but we will be confining our study to these five. The square hand enjoys order and regularity, whilst the conical or artistic hand has a strong tendency towards sensuality and aesthetics. The knotty or philosophical hand belongs to the analyst and meditator whereas the pointed hand is the least practical, revealing a tendency towards the abstract and, generally, indicating that such people should not be in a position of authority. Finally, the spatulate hand's main characteristics are action, movement and energy.

The left hand is used to determine events and character traits and is called the Hand of Destiny. It is the hand of hereditary factors. The other hand shows how your life develops, and what you make of your potential.

For the purpose of this book, the diagrams have been prepared for the left hand in each case to make it easier to locate and identify lines and markings.

On each diagram, the shaded area indicates the part of the hand which is being dealt with.

The Square or Useful hand	
The Conical or Artistic hand	
The Knotty or Philosophical hand	
The Pointed or Psychic hand	
The Spatulate or Active hand	

Doctors, mathematicians, scientists and computer programmers	Square hand	
Artists, actors, singers and orators	Conical hand	
Philosophers, analysts and pure scientists	Knotty hand	
Members of religious orders, clairvoyants and social workers	Pointed hand	
Engineers and mechanics, members of the Armed Forces		

Stubborn and reactionary, with little vision. Family-oriented, tends to take jobs which serve others. Dislikes change.

Loves life and people. Good-humoured and charming but also rather shallow and selfish. Publicity-seeking.

Abhors the grossness of life, believes that the next life will be better than this. Remote and ascetic, idealistic and critical.

Quiet nature, loving beauty and living on an exalted emotional level. Easily hurt, good intuition and often academically bright.

Restless and indecisive, this practical and inventive person dreams obsessively of the future and constantly thinks up new ideas and concepts.

COLOUR OF THE PALM

Very pale skin on palm	Selfish and could suffer from bad circulation
Yellow skin on palm	Morbid and could suffer from bilious attacks
Pink and mottled skin on palm	Cheerful disposition, well-balanced
Red skin on palm	Quick-tempered
Very red skin on palm	Violent disposition, should watch blood pressure
Silky skin on palm	Tendency to rheumatism and gout
Dry skin on palm	Runs temperatures easily, prone to fevers
Damp skin on palm	Ill-balanced moral nature, prone to liver and kidney disorders

HAIR ON THE HAND

Hairy hands on a woman – mannish and cruel

Hairy hands on a man – energetic and sexy

Very hairy hands on a man – violent nature

No hair on a man's hands – effeminate and passive

Light-coloured hair on hands – passionless

Dark hair on hands – passionate disposition

Reddish-coloured hair on hands – excitable nature

Air sign	Aquarius Gemini Libra	Round hands with Conic type fingers
Fire sign	Aries Leo Sagittarius	Long hands with short thick fingers
Water sign	Pisces Cancer Scorpio	Long hands with long thin fingers
Earth sign	Taurus Virgo Capricorn	Square hands with short square fingers

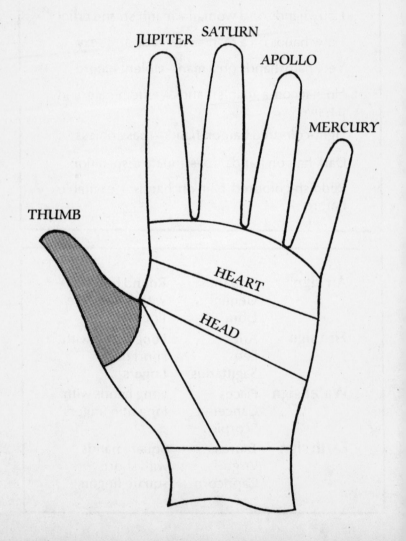

THE THUMB

The Thumb or 'Thenar Eminence' is the most important digit on the hand; without it one would find it difficult to cope with everyday living. It also has the most significant meaning in reading hands. The main thing to remember is that the thumb represents one's self-control and to some extent the control of others. The thumb must be adequately proportioned in relation to the hand or there will be insufficient firmness of purpose.

The thumb has three phalanges and not two as is commonly supposed. The upper nail phalange determines the will, the middle phalange logic and reason, and the lower phalange, which is the Mount of Venus, love, energy and sympathy.

A longer thumb in comparison with the other fingers suggests a person who is out to impress, and who is, at the same time, impressionable. People in high places, such as Prime Ministers, tend to have noticeably large thumbs.

A short stunted thumb betrays a lack of will, swinging moods and an outlook which is not based on logic. A short thick thumb implies primitive taste, and a person who is uncouth, albeit blunt and honest. If, however, the thumb is proportionately long, then thickness shows health and vitality. Thin thumbs indicate a nervous disposition.

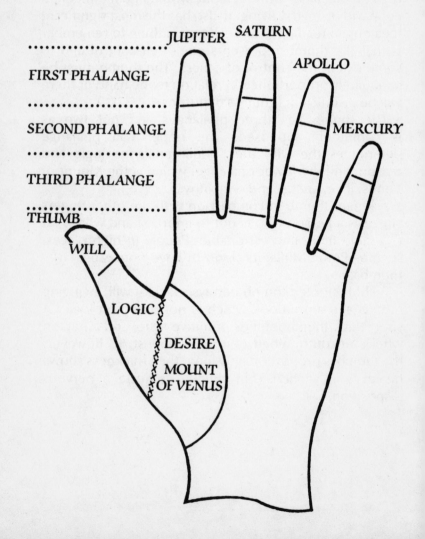

Fun-loving	45° to Jupiter	
Wants to impress people	90° to Jupiter, and large	
Sycophantic	Close to hand	
Overbearing	Thick	
Rather cold and distant	Medium	

Generous and tends towards extremes	90° to Jupiter	
Snake in the grass	Long and close to hand	
Pervertedly cruel	Short, thick and chubby	
Bad-tempered	Short	
Refined	Thin	

Impulsive	Conic	
Violent tendencies: the Murderer's Thumb	Short, chubbed	
Practical	Square top	
Weak-willed	Short	

Very determined	Long, strong and broad	
Strong will-power	Long	
Craves excitement; an extrovert	Angled over	
Obstinate	Narrowing	
Under stress	Horizontal bars	

Logical	Second phalange equal to first	
Diplomatic and unbearably charming	Second phalange longer than first and thin	
Reasonable and never brutish	Much longer than first phalange	
Loves family life; egocentric	Family Ring	
Excellent timing and patience; good musician, orator or sportsman	Angle of Time	

Very sensitive and easily upset; afraid of marriage	Line running across	
Boasts openly and crudely about love-life; could have an incestuous relationship	Crosses on Venus	
Easily upset and totally unpredictable; has select but strong friendships	Jointy or knotty	
Acts on instinct and intuition, won't listen to logical arguments	Short	
Argumentative and violent; avoid conflicts with such a person	Very short	

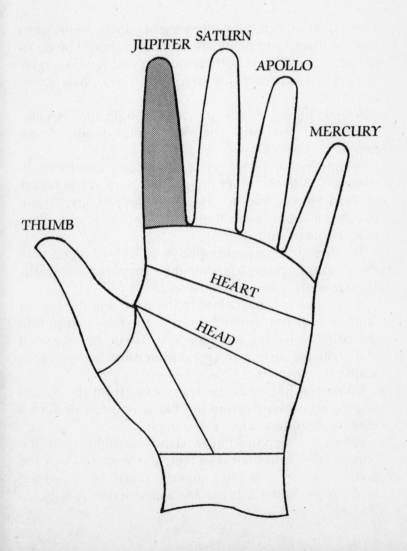

THE JUPITER OR INDEX FINGER

The Jupiter or index finger represents pride, self-esteem and the capacity to dominate. Its length should be equal to that of Apollo and both the Jupiter and Apollo fingers should at least reach the base of the top phalange of Saturn.

A poor Jupiter finger, shorter in length than Apollo, denotes an inferiority complex – short Jupiter finger people do not like responsibility.

When the Jupiter finger is large, long and heavy in comparison to the other fingers, the person has power to lead others and to assume responsibility. These people like to feel important and are therefore susceptible to flattery.

The Jupiter finger must always be judged along with the thumb because together they show the conscious attitude of the person to the world.

If the thumb is held close to the hand and the Jupiter finger stands out, while the rest of the fingers turn into the palm, you have a person who is socially awkward and unadaptable but with great pretension and power to realise their potential.

When the Jupiter finger leans away from the Saturn finger and outwards from the hand, one can deduce a very strong independence of thought.

When the Jupiter finger stands straight then the person stands on their own feet; if it leans towards the Saturn finger (second finger), there is a strong involvement with the home and a love of domesticity.

Ambitious and not afraid to take responsibility	Large and heavy	
Very studious	Straight, long and knotty	
Bossy and domineering	Pointed	
Good company; unconventional	Isolated	
Happy as a bachelor; wise	Solomon's Ring	

Hates responsibility	Shorter than Apollo
Lack of self-esteem	Bent, withered
Wilful	Inclined to Saturn
Has difficulty relating to others	Gap between Jupiter and Saturn
Withdrawn	Short

Spiritual	Fleshy	
Likely to be involved in politics; very religious	Long	
Great orator or politician	Very big	
May not have many genuine friends	Dry and thin	
Bossy	Pointed	

Love of self	Plump and short	
Charitable and caring but weak-willed	Short	
Rheumatic, prone to gout	Top phalange inclines to Saturn	

Desire for recognition	Long	
Very subjective	Jointy or knotty	
Excellent cook	Plump	
Glutton	Fat	
Martyr-like withdrawal	Thin	

Dominant and materialistic	Long	
Desire for glory, domination	Thin	
Material ambition	Plump	
Order in personal things	Jointy	
Realistic	Long and thin	

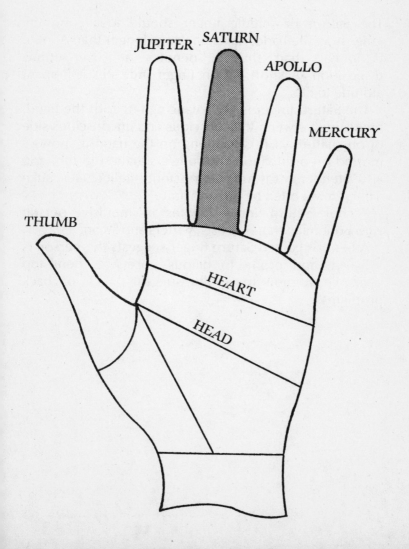

THE SATURN OR MIDDLE FINGER

The Saturn or middle finger should ideally be the longest on the hand, half a phalange longer than Apollo. If longer than this, it denotes an over-serious disposition. A short Saturn finger indicates a flippant attitude to life.

The Saturn finger is the balancing finger of the hand, mediating between the conscious and unconscious side of our nature. If it is too long on the hand it shows a morbid preoccupation with one's situation in life, and also a tendency towards depression. Intellectually, such a person will often be out on a limb.

A short Saturn finger denotes an impulsive person with Bohemian traits – artists, writers and so on.

A bent or curved Saturn finger suggests the person is sensitive and prone to bilious upsets. A bent top phalange turning to Apollo suggests neck or back problems.

Prone to depression	Heavy and broad	
Loyal, serious	Longest on hand	
Perceptive	Bends back	
Unable to face up to life	Bends in	
Harbours a guilty secret	Saturn and Apollo wilt towards each other	

An intellectual who may be less than sparkling socially	Leans to Apollo	
Flippant	Thin	
Morbid outlook on life	Heavy	
Prone to spine trouble	Crooked	
Non-achiever	Short	

Natural gift for clairvoyance	Long and fleshy	
Loves magic, mystery and freemasonry	Long	
Psychic	Pointed	
An accurate judge of others; good at figure work and music	Square top	
Can be too serious about the occult – a fanatic!	Thin	

Mystical	Conical top	
Bad at figure work	Short, pointed	
Influenced by superficial considerations	Short	
Interested in the occult	Large and heavy	

Very good director of scientific projects	Jointy or knotty	
Very scientific	Long	
Will see a project to its end	Thin	
Can't see beyond theory	Plump	
Finds it difficult to complete tasks	Short	

Greenfingers	Long	
Cut off from reality	Ringed	
Lazy and rather parasitic	Fleshy	
Spendthrift	Thin	
Poor money sense	Short	

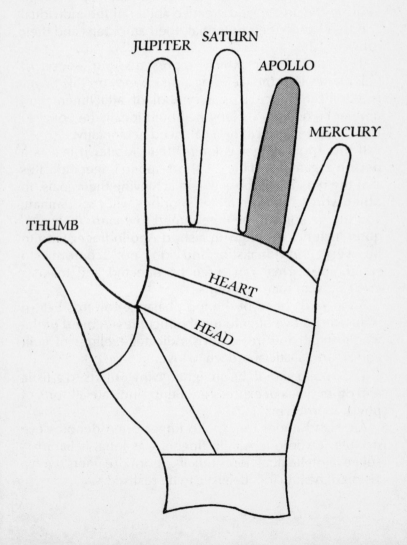

THE APOLLO OR SUN FINGER

The Apollo or Sun finger is traditionally supposed to indicate the artistic and creative ability of the individual and to relate to their potential, their ambitions and their future wealth.

It is this finger which represents our sense of belonging. That the wedding ring is worn on this finger is significant since it is a symbol of attachment and mutual belonging. Its length should ideally be equal to that of Jupiter, indicating a balanced personality.

If the Apollo finger is longer than Jupiter it makes a person a 'gambler of life'. A short Apollo finger indicates that the person will be active in achieving their goals. In other words, the Jupitarian emotions will predominate and the person will be determined to ensure their own good fortune. People with a short Apollo finger tend to be very individualistic and do not conform to stereotypes. They can often be affected and make a great show of their emotions.

An inwards bend of the top phalange towards Saturn is also indicative of emotional difficulties. A bend of the whole finger towards Saturn indicates feelings of guilt and an unrealistic approach to love.

The Apollo should be straight, giving outlets to artistic and other types of expression. Bends indicate all sorts of physical problems.

An island under the Apollo finger often denotes eye trouble. Over-long Apollo fingers – as long as Saturn – suggest intellectual bores but also born dreamers, with a vision of beauty too idealistic to be realised.

Balanced personality	Equal to Jupiter	
Sunny disposition	Straight	
Will take risks	Longer than Jupiter	
Needs to marry an older person	Wilts to Saturn	
Great artistic potential	Long with spatulate tip	

Hidden sorrow	Bent over	
Cautious, never gambles with life	Shorter than Jupiter	
Could be spiritual leader	Clings to Mercury	
Should take more exercise	Crooked	
Riddled with guilt	Clings to Saturn	

An intellectual person with an interest in art	Long	
Sensitivity of thought in artistic matters; refined	Thin	
Love of beauty in all forms	Plump	
Good taste	Conic	
Enigmatic	Pointed	

Destroys and never rebuilds	Jointy or knotty	
Lacks breeding	Square	
Lacks finesse	Short	

Skilled at translating ideas into concrete form	Plump	
By dint of hard work this person will usually succeed	Long	
Idealistic, artistic and precise	Thin	
This person has a need for beauty and order in their life	Jointy or knotty	

Yearns for riches and likes to be surrounded by art	Long	
A perfectionist	Jointy or knotty	
Little respect for fame and money	Thin	
Remarkably bad taste and ostentatious too!	Plump	
One of the less refined types; likely to fail, especially if the task requires artistic talent	Short	

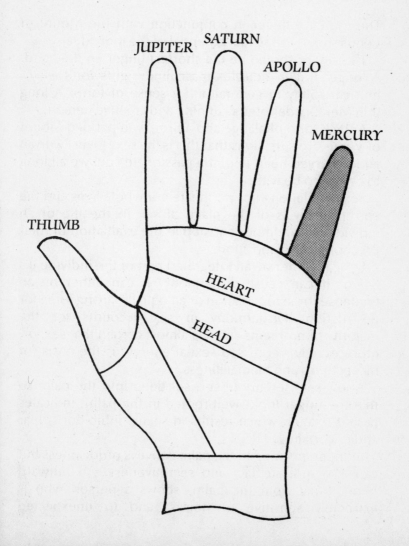

THE MERCURY OR LITTLE FINGER

The Mercury finger in conjunction with the Mount of Venus shows the sexual potential of the individual.

This finger should be the shortest finger on the hand. A longer finger indicates masculinity, gifts for speech, musical ability in general and a sense of form. A long thin Mercury denotes a cunning and creative person.

A thick third phalange and a firm, well-padded Mount of Venus are sure signs that this is the sexy lover; with an added curved heart line, the passionate soul we all long to be – or to be with.

Sexual relationships permeate our whole lives and the correct analysis of the place of sex in the life of an individual is an important step in the evaluation of their psychological disposition.

Sex can either be an integrated part of the individual's life or it can cause disharmony. It can either be an immense force for creation or an equally strong force for destruction. Disharmony in sex accounts for the majority of problems and it is almost certain that sex, or, more exactly, repressed sexual energy, is the basis for most crimes and mental illness.

A low-set Mercury finger, set deep into the palm so that the finger looks well-rooted in the palm, indicates parent fixation which results in sexual inhibitions, fear and uncertainty.

A finger inclining to the palm conveys prudishness but can also indicate tact and secretiveness. An outward bend, away from the palm, shows a person who is extremely sensitive to noises, and to unexpected reactions to the environment.

A broad, physical finger shows a broad mind. A plump Mercury is for a person who understands business and knows how to make money.

The Mercury finger is the only finger without a nail moon. If there is one it will disappear early in life.

A Mercury finger which arcs towards Apollo shows self-sacrifice and a person well-suited to the caring professions.

Thrives on knowledge; excellent hearing	Long with long first phalange	
Very sexy, and fulfilled in all aspects of life	Thick base and knotty joints	
A cunning mind; clever and successful negotiator	Long	
Self-sacrificing nature makes them ideal as nurses or doctors	Curved towards Apollo	
Sublimates their sexual urge into a money-making drive	Ring	

Avoids commitment to relationships, prefers to keep a distance	Wide apart from Apollo	
Tactful and secretive	Clings to Apollo	
Longs for affection	Clings to hand	
May be rather immature or even retarded	Shorter than second phalange of Apollo	
Intellectual	Halfway up first Apollo phalange	

Gift for languages	Jointy or knotty	
Flair for business	Thin	
Ability for science	Long	
Will make a good and lasting marriage	One line	
More than one love	More than one line	

Great at listening and giving advice	Several lines: 'Samaritan lines'	
Teeth need attention	Straight lines under Mercury	
Excellent hearing	Pointed	
Little finesse	Plump	
Intellectual bore	Short	

Natural gift for business or law	Jointy or knotty	
Gift for making money	Thick	
Practical and materialistic	Long	
Unrealistic	Thin	
Always tired	Lines going down	

Good sex life	Plump	
Cunning and hypocritical; likely to be a charlatan	Long	
Has problems achieving orgasm	Ringed	
May find it difficult to relate to parents, one of whom may come from another country	Low set	
Poor sex life	Flat	

Frustrated	Thin
Stupid	Short

THE NAILS

The nails are most informative. For instance, we all know that people who bite their nails show a nervous disposition. Flecks on the nails donate a tired, run-down condition. Short nails which are broader than they are long show a stubborn nature. Broad, long nails indicate clear judgement. Long, almond-shaped nails suggest a less energetic person, whilst white nails show a cold nature. Long, ridged nails, bluish in colour, betray problems. Brittle nails with the first phalange of the index finger (the 'Jupiter' finger) inclining reveal gout.

•CHIROMANCY•

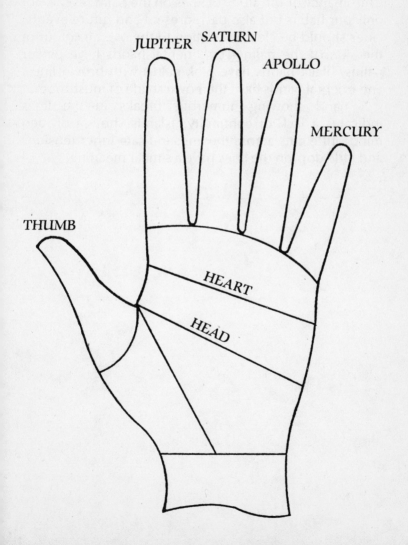

LINES ON THE HAND

Chiromancy or the study of lines on the palm reveals not only our habits but also past, present and future events. Lines should be clear in relation to the overall colour of the skin of the palm – continental hands have pinker palms, black hands have pink palms with brown lines, and oriental hands have their own shade of mushroom.

A hand showing numerous breaks in the lines indicates a lack of continuity; islands show a divided mind; little cuts across the lines indicate inner tensions and little dots on the lines have a similar meaning.

THE MAIN LINES ON THE HAND

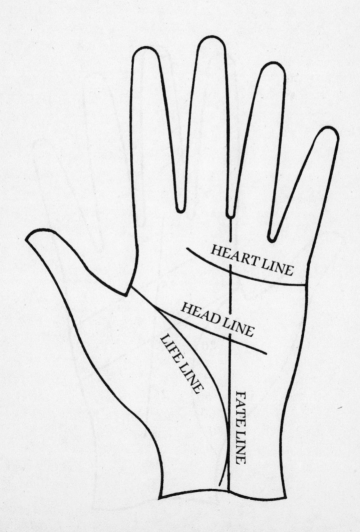

HEART LINE

HEAD LINE

LIFE LINE

FATE LINE

TIME ON THE HAND

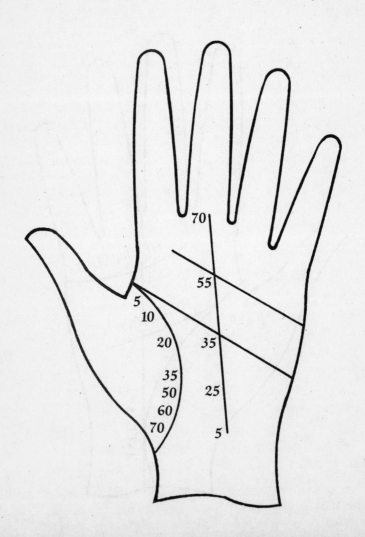

THE HEART LINE

Read from below the Mount of Mercury across the hand, this represents the unconscious expression of emotions, the circulation, and the affections.

It also suggests the sexual motivation of the person; the straighter the line, the more 'feminine' and the more calculating. The deeper the curve, the more 'masculine' and the more forceful the feelings.

If the line is made up of uneven chains, the person has a normal sexual appetite. If it runs straight across the hand this is an indication of jealousy due to excesses of affection. Breaks in the heart line show great inconstancy in relationships and, on man's hand, often indicate a woman-hater.

White marks on the line show love affairs; red spots on or gaps in the line represent physical or emotional wounds.

This fair-weather friend is fickle, inconstant and vain; don't take your problems to them	Broken line	
Jealous, possessive and selfish in love; quick to anger, slow to forgive; will never see your point of view	Long, straight heart line	
Prone to illness and allergy, always under emotional strain; complains a lot	Even-chained heart line	
Impatient in life and love; emotionally over the top	Deep, long heart line	
Miserly and rather selfish	Short and faint	

A great lover and a flirt, boundless charm	Branches on heart line	
Always more than just a friend; hot-blooded and passionate but easily upset	Ideal heart line	
Sincere and warm, will make close friendships and will always be very understanding	Set low beneath fingers	
Too charming to be true; a smooth, impenetrable exterior hides shallow emotions	Tram lines	
A closed, defensive character who is difficult to get to know; the island hints at a guilty secret	Island on line	

THE HEAD LINE

The head line represents the conscious and unconscious thought processes.

The straighter and shorter the line, the less likely the person is to be an initiator.

Straight with a sudden drop shows extremes of moods, sudden and unexpected, which can make a person seem thoughtless and cruel.

The line should suit the type of hand – a damaged line can suggest a tendency to alcoholism; too fine a line, an explosive situation; too broad, no energy to back up ideas; low on the hand and curved, passionate thoughts. The deeper the line towards the Moon Mount, the more imagination and fantasy.

Modest and likeable; a good all-rounder with a steady success rate	Ideal head line, lightly attached to life line	
Imaginative and creative with a particular skill for one art; may have suicidal tendencies	Deeper dip to Moon Mount	
Very down to earth; will always attempt to be objective	Follows own course	
Friends are merely contacts in this type's ceaseless search for money	Sharp upturn towards Mercury	
Combines imagination and practicality; very good listener	'Writer's fork' on head line	

Hurtful, poor self-control, rather dull	Gap at beginning of life line from head line	
The islands indicate times of great strain which this type will avoid if at all possible	Islands on head line	
Lacks self-confidence, very critical of own failings	Turning down	
Finds it difficult to take criticism and is generally of a nervous disposition	Barbed	
Lacking in confidence, unaware of own potential, too quick to agree with others	Tied to life line with short Jupiter finger	

THE LIFE LINE

Usually this line is long, completely encircling the Mount of Venus. It is used to determine time in a person's life and is divided up into periods of five and ten years.

Like all the major lines on the hand, it will differ from person to person. A short life line *does not* necessarily mean a short life, but does usually mean that the person has wasted their life and has not followed their true destiny.

Reckless and hysterical	Wide gap between beginning of life line and head line	
More evenly balanced and easier approach to life	Head line joining life line at beginning	
Cautious, lacks self-confidence	Head line tied to life line into palm	
Change	Break in life line	
Planned change	Overlapping break in life line	

Tries too hard	Life line etched deeply into palm	
Good health, success and financial benefits	Small branches running upwards on each side of life line	
Warning of financial losses; poor health	Small branches running down: 'dropping lines'	
Very good health, plenty of energy	Double life line	
Heavily influenced by the family	Life line connected to the fate line	

Tapeworm present at time indicated (see Time Chart p.72)	Blue spot on life line	
Great healing power	Square on life line	
Wasted, not necessarily a short, life	Short life line	
Bilious constitution	Island on life line	

THE FATE LINE

The fate line normally ends at the top of the hand below the fingers. A woman's hand without a fate line means she has an unstressful life and can afford to be very feminine, in the traditional sense of not having a career, because she has responsibility taken away from her by a man.

This isn't often the case today as women have to work, so the fate line is generally deep and strong – showing women are heavily involved in life and work.

Men should show a fate line as it indicates direction in life. The point where it starts indicates the beginning of a career and the point where it ends shows the final destination of their life.

Unlucky in love; may take early retirement	Fate line ending at heart line	
Lives a life of great variety with much travel; wealth is dependent on someone of the opposite sex	Fate line starting from Moon Mount to Saturn finger	
Ambitious, will achieve power and authority over others	Fate line which runs towards Jupiter	
A sign of good luck, popularity and success; fame and fortune are in the pipeline	Fate line which runs to Apollo	
Science is the key to success for this type; they will be a business tycoon or a well-known scientist	Fate line to Mercury	

Missed chances to develop natural gifts in early years of life	Fate line from life line to Saturn	
Positive approach to life Uncertain approach to life	Strong fate line Faint fate line	
Forced to assume position of responsibility at an early age	Fate line starting from wrist to Saturn	
Family is a helpful influence; an excellent start to life	Fate line from Mount of Venus to Saturn	
As a result of their own efforts, will become successful from the age of 35 onwards	Fate line from head line to Saturn	

Success and prosperity will be gradually achieved	Fate line with rising lines	
Warning of loss of money and possessions	Fate line with lines dropping	
Bad start or bad end to life; hardship	Fate line crossed or chained at start or end	
Change at time indicated (see Time Chart p.72)	Cross alongside fate line	
Unlucky omen; warns against financial loss	Cross on fate line	

An influence coming into life such as a close relationship	Influence line coming up to fate line	
A source of protection	Square on fate line	
Planned change	Overlapping line on fate line	
Unforeseen change in life	Broken fate line	

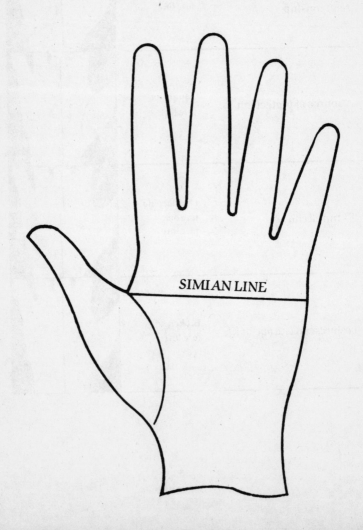

SIMIAN LINE

THE SIMIAN LINE

The Simian line runs horizontally across the palm and is the head and heart line combined.

It is rarely found on both the left *and* right hand. When found on both hands it denotes a person high in a religious order and a potential genius.

When the Simian line appears on the left hand only it usually implies a high intellect, a difficult disposition and is often associated with great disappointments in life.

When the Simian line appears on the right hand only it shows great intensity of being, a selfish and treacherous nature – someone who could be a hypocrite and who achieves their successes at the cost of others.

MOUNTS ON THE HAND

The Mounts are the highest fleshy parts in the hand. These Mounts are named after the seven principal planets and each Mount has certain characteristics. They are as follows:

The Mount of Venus:	Sensuality, passion, love
The Mount of Jupiter:	Domination, power, ambition
The Mount of Saturn:	Melancholy, seriousness, withdrawal
The Mount of Apollo:	Brilliance, success
The Mount of Mercury:	Commerce, science, mortality
The Mount of Mars:	Courage and vitality
The Moon Mount:	Changeability, romance, imagination

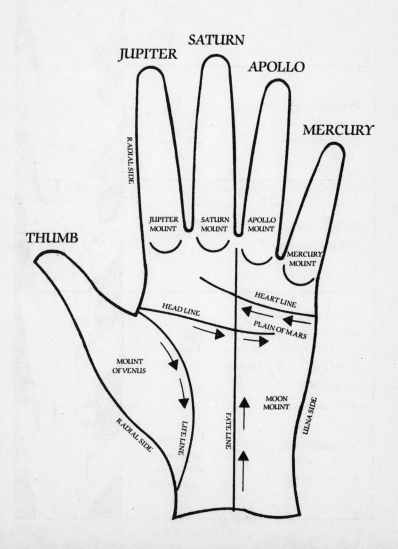

Love affair which must be kept secret because one partner is married	Line running from Venus through life, head and heart lines	
Person who keeps two affairs going at the same time	Two lines running from Venus to star on fate line	
Full-blooded and passionate	Many crosses on Mount of Venus	
Somebody is exerting a powerful influence – the nearer the influence line is the life line, the stronger the influence	Influence line running close to life line	
A good omen; great achievement will bring rich rewards	Line from Venus ending with a star under Jupiter	

Represents our capacity for love and friendship; appreciation of beauty	Fleshy ball at base of thumb	
Warm, uncritical, and sexy; attracted to opposite sex; adores children	Broad, firm and rounded	
Cold and suspicious with a pessimistic outlook; not very attractive sexually, poor health in general	Narrow and flat	
On right hand, people one likes; on left hand, people who like you	Influence lines running parallel to life line	
Symbol of great charm, luck in love and sex appeal	Star in middle of Mount of Venus	

LINES ON THE HAND FROM THE MOUNT OF VENUS

Wealth will come as a result of family help	Line from Venus to Saturn	
A very lucky line denoting wealth, fame and influential associates	Line from Venus to Apollo	
Any chance of success is undermined	Line cuts through into Apollo finger	
Achievement in business of scientific pursuits	Line from Venus to Mercury	
Denotes greed and a love of luxury	Soft, fleshy Mount of Venus	

A marriage or relationship will dominate an entire lifetime	Star just under base of thumb	
Difficulties in path to true love	Star at base of Venus	
Denotes a calculating attitude and a marriage made for money and status	Triangle on Mount of Venus	
One love only in life	One large cross	
Denotes the influence of loved ones	Lines running across Venus	

Sensual indulgence or unnatural vice will be uncovered	Star low down on Mount of Venus	
Two simultaneous love affairs – one will end in disaster	Two lines from Mount of Venus to Mercury	
Perfect health and a long life	Double life line	
Excess of tenderness	Branches at beginning and end of heart line	
Hysterical emotions and unusually intense attachments	Two lines beginning from centre of Venus and joining on palm	

LINES ON THE HAND TO AND FROM THE MOUNT OF APOLLO

Will achieve recognition for success helped by devotion of family	*Line from life line to Apollo*	
Success and honour by own merit in whatever occupation is taken up	*Line from fate line to Apollo*	
Success and fame in any occupation	*'Sun line' – line from wrist to Apollo*	
This line indicates success in life and especially in love	*Line from Moon Mount to Apollo*	
May mean suffering in old age but also indicates a marriage or close relationship late in life	*Apollo line to heart line*	

Success in later life, but accompanied by bitterness	Large star under Apollo	
Realisation of ambitions	'Tree of Success' – tree under Apollo	
Sense of humour	Loop under Apollo	
Recognition in middle age due to own efforts	Apollo line to head line	
Shock	Small star on Apollo line	
Hardship	Bars across	
Scandal	Island	
Protection	Square	

Success line	Line to heart line under Apollo	
Success in two different careers or activities	Two lines from Apollo to heart line	
Achievement of aims	'Tree of success' from beneath Apollo to heart line	

THE HEALTH OR LIVER LINE

The health or liver line originates on the Moon Mount towards Mercury. When it is well-traced it denotes a good stomach.

When it is not traced on the hand it suggests great agility. It also indicates a tight-closed skin which does not sweat; it makes the person more prone to headaches and migraines.

A liver line which is discoloured, brown or yellow, suggests a liverish person who is bad-tempered and irritable.

The healthiest hands have no health line; the deeper the line is etched, the more serious the condition	Deep line	
Bilious attacks; if the line cuts through head line stress is present	Wavy or brownish health line	
Infertility or complications in childbirth	Star	
Lung trouble	Many islands on health line	
Sign of healing and protection in health	Square on health line	

THE THREE BRACELETS OR RASCETTES

These should be three clearly traced lines at the base of the palm which denote health, wealth and good luck respectively. They are sometimes known as the 'bracelets of life' and they are said to be the indication of 25-30 years of life, respectively.

Health	First bracelet	
Wealth	Second bracelet	
Happiness	Third bracelet	
Happiness in old age	More than three bracelets	
Possibility of miscarriage	Light, short, acute line from top bracelet	
Abortion	Short, dark, acute line from top bracelet	
Empty life	No bracelets	

Struggles, hard work and worries but success will come eventually	First bracelet chained or islanded	
In a woman's hand, high uterus and difficulty in becoming pregnant	First bracelet arching into palm	
Mother had difficulty in having you (left hand); difficulty in having own baby (right hand)	First bracelet deep in colour	
A legacy can be expected	Star in middle of top bracelet	

Again, this can indicate an inheritance	Angle in top bracelet	
Will have some difficulties in life; situation will improve in middle years	Cross in top bracelet	
Sudden wealth	Line from bracelet to Mercury	
Money problems throughout life	Second bracelet chained	

THE GIRDLE OF VENUS

In actual fact, a hand has a better reading without the Girdle of Venus. It always denotes a craving for excitement, a hysterical, nervous nature, and a tendency towards acute depression.

A normal Girdle of Venus starts between the first and second fingers and ends between the third and fourth fingers.

A very deep, red line suggests the person will have vicious tendencies and their career will suffer because of this. On no account should they consider a career in medicine.

A very thin line suggests the person will be talented in literature, have a strong will-power and a generally pleasant disposition.

A double or triple Girdle of Venus indicates bad features in the character, increasing in proportion to the number of lines. The Girdle of Venus is associated with vices and bad habits.

The ancients considered the Girdle of Venus to be an undesirable sign on the hand, unless there were several of them, or it showed significant markings (see diagrams). Today it is simply thought of as a sign of craving for excitement. If it is joined all the way along with no breaks, then the longing for excitement will never be satisfied.

Person has straight forward human passions	Normal Girdle of Venus	
A tendency to be hysterical	Double Girdle of Venus	
Venereal disease	Triple, shredded Girdle around Saturn	
An erotic nature	Girdle of Venus cut through by small lines	

UNUSUAL MARKINGS

Eye problems	Circle on life line	
Outstanding success in career	Circle on Mount of Apollo	
Protection from accidents	Square on Venus	
Could serve term of imprisonment	Large square on Venus	
Unhappiness caused by love	Star on Mount of Venus	

Military honour	Star on Plain of Mars	
Kleptomaniac	Star on Mount of Mercury	
Ill-fated wealth, fortune which brings unhappiness	Star on Mount of Apollo	
Death by the scaffold*	Star on Mount of Saturn	
One capable of murder	Symbol on Mount of Venus with short, thick tip to thumb	

(*old reading)

An amorous but inconstant disposition	Many lines encircling base of thumb	
Honour and distinction, unexpected glory	Star on Mount of Jupiter	
One good marriage	One cross on Mount of Jupiter	
Two good marriages	Two crosses on Mount of Jupiter	
Riches achieved by own endeavours	Grille on second phalange of Jupiter	
Capable of adultery	Grille on third phalange of Jupiter	

Highly successful in marriage; great insight into others' minds	Cross under Jupiter	
Loves to have palm read	Cross under Mercury	
Wise, knows how to exercise power; need never marry	Ring round Jupiter	
Great gift for clairvoyance or second sight	A figure eight beginning the fate line	

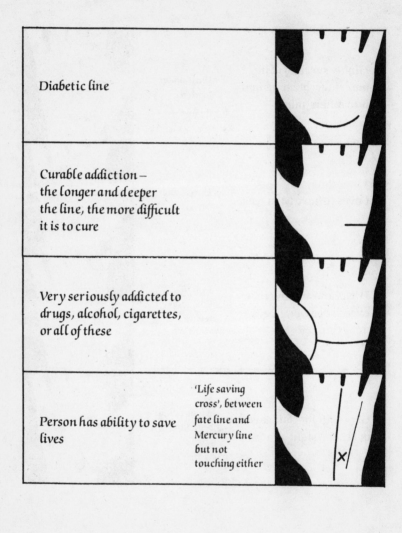

Diabetic line	
Curable addiction – the longer and deeper the line, the more difficult it is to cure	
Very seriously addicted to drugs, alcohol, cigarettes, or all of these	
Person has ability to save lives	'Life saving cross', between fate line and Mercury line but not touching either

A cowardly and mean disposition	Small triangle	
Can bear physical pain	Narrow triangle with hard, rough skin	
Business will be a failure	Narrow triangle and poor head line	
Spendthrift	Bulging on Plain of Mars	

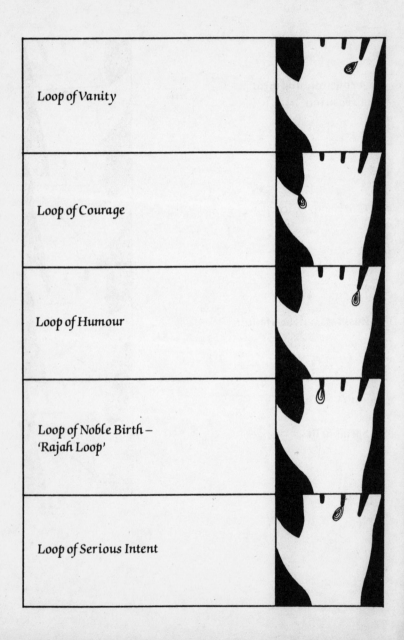

Loop of Vanity

Loop of Courage

Loop of Humour

Loop of Noble Birth –
'Rajah Loop'

Loop of Serious Intent

Love of Music	Loops at base of Venus	
Loop of Good Memory		
Loop of Humanism		

●DERMATOGLYPHICS●

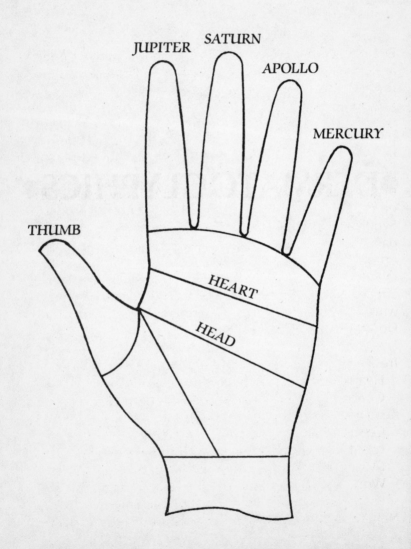

SKIN PATTERNS OR DERMATOGLYPHICS

Dermatoglyphics is the name given to the study of ridge and furrow patterns on the palms and on the soles of the feet. (Derma is the Greek word for skin.)

Each person's skin pattern is totally unique, a fact which is upheld by the important use the police make of fingerprint patterns in identifying criminals. **Derma-**toglyphics is also used extensively in the fields of genetics and medicine. More specifically, a great variety of problems relating to chromosome abnormalities can be detected in this way. One such example is Down's Syndrome (mongolism) where the palm and sole ridge patterns are very definitely different from those of a normal person. Similarly, distinctive peculiarities occur in the dermatoglyphs of people with sex chromosome abnormalities. Today, research workers can recognise with certainty the prints of ninety-five per cent of all Down's Syndrome babies.

Medical research has found that certain diseases frequently manifest themselves on the palm as follows:

Heart disease – Heart line thin and dotted

Gonorrhoea – Broken down skin pattern and islanded head line

Colitis – Split fate line and islanded life line

Cystitis – Islanded lines and malformed patterns

Low blood pressure – Very flexible hands

Work on the study of the skin began in the seventeenth century and in 1684 an English doctor, Nehemiah Grew, published a paper for the Royal Society of Medicine on his findings regarding ridges and patterns on the palm and fingers. Various other theories followed – in 1892 Sir Francis Galton published a book *Fingerprints* which laid the foundations for what we know as Dermatoglyphics.

On both the hands and the feet ridges run in different directions and cover different areas. There are three types of pattern found on the fingertips – the arch, the loop and the whorl. There are differences between the sexes and races; women, for instance, seem to have narrower ridges than men.

After severe burning which necessitates skin grafts, the patterns have been known to reappear in their original form after healing.

Physiologically speaking, the linear formations found on the epidermis of the hand serve a three-fold purpose. They act as secretion channels for the sweat, they form a rough surface to aid gripping, and they form a corrugated texture which heightens the stimulation of the nerve endings beneath the epidermis and facilitates tactile sensitivity. Epidermal ridges are developed in the foetus by the eighteenth week of pregnancy and the individual pattern formation remains without natural change until death.

The reading will vary according to where the peacock's eye is positioned. When it is high towards the tip of the finger, the subject will have high ideals, abstract thoughts and theories. When it is low down towards the base of the finger, a physical and practical approach will be found. When it is in the centre, the effect will be that of a well-balanced individual who is able to give their thoughts free expression.

Determined but not stubborn	Tented arch	
Very persistent will-power	Whorl	
Secretive nature	Whorl (on all digits)	
Knows own mind	Loop	
Hesitant	Composite	

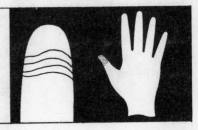

Tendency to categorise people

Arch

RINGS ON THE HAND

Rings worn on the thumb denote an ego-centric personality.

Rings worn on the Jupiter finger indicate a person wishing to dominate.

Rings worn on the Saturn finger suggest a serious-minded person.

Rings worn on the Apollo finger disclose a person influenced by the superficial aspects of life who has no time for deeper feelings.

Rings worn on the left-hand Mercury finger show the possessor has a sexual obsession or complex. The heavier and flashier the ring, the coarser the complex.

Rings worn on the right-hand Mercury finger show a sublimated sexual urge, diverted into making money, and are therefore often found on business men.

Good legal mind, can see both sides of an argument	Composite	
Practical person, good manager	Radial loop	
Skilled in business but not destined for the top	Loops	
Should work in communication	Whorl	
Devoted to causes, could be a nurse	Tent	

Self-determined	Whorl		
Open-minded in metaphysical matters	Loops		
Combines the spiritual and the material, practical yet dreamy	Composite		
Desires pomp and circumstance	Arch		
Follower of 'isms'	Tented arch		

Gift for music	Tented arch		
Charming with close friends, but otherwise tough and earthy	Composite		
Individualistic, artistic	Whorl		
Appreciative of new ideas in fashion	Loops		
Conforms to standards	Arch		

PATTERNS ON THE MERCURY FINGER

Ninety per cent of Mercury fingerprint patterns are loops. It is the ideal pattern for this finger. It denotes humour and freedom in all forms of expression, as well as aiding harmony in working with other people. Loops always turn towards the Ulna side of the hand.

Whorls on Mercury show sincerity in everything that is undertaken. When the subject feels strongly about a topic they will defend their viewpoint passionately.

Arches on the Mercury finger tend to restrict artistic expression.

BIBLIOGRAPHY

Having read this book and, we hope, become more interested in the whole subject of palmistry, you might like to consider reading further publications on this topic. Here is a suggested reading list which will provide some starting-points.

Henry Frith, *Palmistry, Secrets Revealed*
(Ward Lock 1952)

Louise Owen (editor of revised edition),
Cheiro – You and Your Hand (Jarrolds – 1969)

Jo Sheridan, *What Your Hands Reveal* (Arco 1963)

Walter Sorell, *The Story of the Human Hand*
(Weidenfeld and Nicolson 1968)

J.Spier, *The Hands of Children*
(Routledge and Kegan , Paul 1955)

Dr. Charlotte Wolff, *Studies in Hand Reading*
(Methuen 1951)